CHAPTER 1
LEWIS & CLARK

The brand new United States is on shaky ground -- most of its towns are east of the **Appalachian Mountains**, along the Atlantic seaboard. **France** and **Great Britain** are the most powerful nations in the world, and both have claims on big sections of the **North American continent** to the north and west of the U.S. But suddenly French leader **Napoleon** makes an offer that will change the direction of the new nation . . .

WHO PURCHASED LOUISIANA LAND?

WASHINGTON, D.C., IN 1803: TWO VIRGINIANS ARE IN THE PRESIDENT'S MANSION...

UM, PRESIDENT JEFFERSON?

BANG KPOW

YES, YES, MERIWETHER, WHAT IS IT NOW?? BANG

EEK! YA GOT ME!

A TOP-SECRET MESSAGE FROM FRENCH EMPEROR **NAPOLEON!**

GOOD! HAS HE AGREED TO MY OFFER TO BUY NEW ORLEANS FROM HIM?

From the desk of NAPOLEON

YOU CAN HAVE NEW ORLEANS — AND THE REST OF THAT WASTELAND CALLED **LOUISIANA!** I AM TOO BUSY FIGHTING THE BRITISH IN EUROPE AND SLAVES IN HAITI TO GUARD THAT LAND. BUY OUR CLAIM ON IT FOR $15 MILLION.

MERIWETHER LEWIS, THIS **LOUISIANA PURCHASE** ADDS 825,000 SQUARE MILES TO THE UNITED STATES! WE **DOUBLE** OUR SIZE!

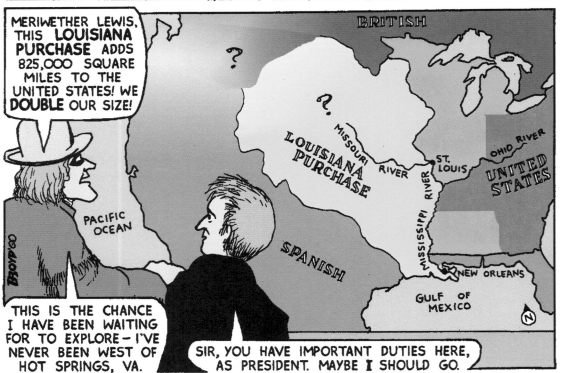

BRITISH

?

?

LOUISIANA PURCHASE

MISSOURI RIVER

ST. LOUIS

OHIO RIVER

UNITED STATES

MISSISSIPPI RIVER

PACIFIC OCEAN

SPANISH

NEW ORLEANS

GULF OF MEXICO

N

THIS IS THE CHANCE I HAVE BEEN WAITING FOR TO EXPLORE — I'VE NEVER BEEN WEST OF HOT SPRINGS, VA.

SIR, YOU HAVE IMPORTANT DUTIES HERE, AS PRESIDENT. MAYBE **I** SHOULD GO.

GOOD POINT! GET A CREW AND TAKE MY FRIEND CHESTER WITH YOU. HE CAN RECORD YOUR DISCOVERIES.

YEAH, WE'VE SEEN YOUR SPELLING, MERIWETHER!

next: PACKING IT IN

WHAT DID LEWIS AND CLARK PACK?

THESE ARE THE VOYAGES OF THE CORPS OF DISCOVERY. ITS THREE-YEAR MISSION: TO SEEK OUT NEW LIFE AND NEW INDIAN CIVILIZATIONS

...TO BOLDLY GO WHERE NO GEEKY WHITE GUYS HAVE GONE BEFORE!!

I AM **NOT** GEEKY! I TRAINED FOR THIS TRIP WITH DOCTORS, SCIENTISTS...

MERIWETHER LEWIS, YOU ARE A GEEK.

OHIO RIVER

I ALSO ASKED MY FORMER COMMANDING OFFICER IN THE ARMY TO JOIN US: WILLIAM CLARK!

MERI! HA! JEFFERSON FINALLY GETS HIS WESTERN TREK. HE BOTHERED MY BROTHER FOR **YEARS** TO EXPLORE THE WEST!

I'VE HIRED A FEW DOZEN GUYS. I'M ALSO BRINGING MY SLAVE, **YORK**. WHAT ARE OUR SUPPLIES?

SUPPLIES INCLUDE RIFLES, LEAD, MEDICINE, DRIED SOUP, AN AIR RIFLE THAT FIRES 40 SHOTS WITHOUT GUNPOWDER, AND A CANOE WITH A 99-POUND FRAME.

DID YOU PACK THE FRUIT ROLLUPS?

BBOYD '00

ON MAY 14, **1804**, THE CORPS LEAVES ST. LOUIS. IT GOES UP THE **MISSOURI RIVER — AGAINST** THE FLOW!

ROW! **ROW!** THIS MAY BE THE FAMOUS NORTHWEST PASSAGE TO THE PACIFIC OCEAN!

YEARRRIGHT. PEOPLE HAVE LOOKED FOR THAT FOR MORE THAN 300 YEARS.

OFTEN THE MEN MUST DRAG THEIR BOATS BECAUSE THE RIVER IS TOO FAST OR FULL OF SANDBARS.

IF THIS IS THE NORTHWEST PASSAGE, IT'S **NOT** WORTH THE TRIP!

next: MAMA SACAGAWEA

WHY DID SACAGAWEA JOIN L & C?

MERIWETHER LEWIS, WILLIAM CLARK, AND CHESTER THE CRAB ARE SAILING UP THE **MISSOURI RIVER** IN 1804...

STOP! WE ARE THE TETON SIOUX. PAY US OR YOU CANNOT TRAVEL BY OUR LAND.

WHAT DO YOU WANT?

ONE OF YOUR BOATS — AND ITS SUPPLIES.

DREAM ON!! WE WILL FIGHT FIRST!

THE TRIBE LETS THE EXPEDITION PASS PEACEFULLY.

I HOPE OTHER INDIANS WE MEET ARE NICER THAN THOSE GUYS!

ME, TOO. WE'RE GOING ONLY 10 MILES A DAY. WINTER IS COMING, AND WE MUST FIND FRIENDLY INDIANS TO CAMP WITH.

ON OCT. 26, LEWIS AND CLARK STOP AT A MANDAN VILLAGE NEAR CANADA.

SURE, YOU CAN LIVE WITH US. BUT YOU WON'T GET OVER THE LARGE MOUNTAINS NEXT SPRING WITHOUT HORSES FROM SHOSHONE TRIBES THAT LIVE THERE.

MY WIFE IS SHOSHONE! WE CAN LEAD YOU WEST!

IN APRIL 1805, THE CORPS OF DISCOVERY GOES WEST AGAIN. IT HAS THREE NEW MEMBERS: FRENCH TRAPPER TOUSSAINT CHARBONNEAU, HIS TEENAGE WIFE SACAGAWEA, AND HER **TWO-MONTH-OLD BABY!**

WAAAAA

UMM, DID WE PACK DIAPERS?

ONE DAY A WIND GUST TIPS ONE OF THE BOATS. SACAGAWEA SAVES BOOKS, CLOTHING, A MAGNET, AND A MICROSCOPE.

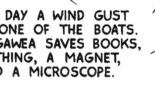

ON MAY 26, THE LEWIS AND CLARK TEAM SEES THE **ROCKY MOUNTAINS.**

THOSE ARE THE "LARGE MOUNTAINS" WE'RE CROSSING?!

uh-oh.

next: EAT AT SHOSHONE's

WHEN DID LEWIS & CLARK GET HOME?

MERIWETHER LEWIS AND WILLIAM CLARK AND THEIR CORPS OF DISCOVERY BUILD FORT CLATSOP TO WAIT OUT WINTER NEAR THE PACIFIC OCEAN IN **1805**.

> DOESN'T THIS RAIN EVER STOP?

> I WOULD NOT CALL THIS "MERRY WEATHER!"

> OH STUFF IT.

ON MARCH 23, 1806, THE EXPLORERS LEAVE THE FORT TO RETURN HOME.

THEY FIND A WAY THROUGH THE **ROCKY MOUNTAINS** THAT IS 600 MILES SHORTER THAN THE PATH THEY TOOK GOING WEST.

> BUT THERE IS NO EASY WAY OVER THIS LAND.

> HEY, WE **ARE** MAKING SOME GREAT MAPS!

ON JULY 27, BLACKFEET INDIANS TRY TO STEAL THEIR GUNS. THE TEAM KILLS TWO — THE ONLY INDIANS KILLED IN THE THREE-YEAR TREK.

ON A SEARCH FOR FOOD ONE DAY, A CREWMAN ACCIDENTALLY HITS LEWIS IN THE BEHIND.

> OW!

> IT'S NO FAIR A GIVING A GUY A SHOT DOWN THERE!!

IN AUGUST 1806, GUIDE SACAGAWEA AND HER FAMILY RETURN HOME TO THE MANDAN INDIANS. ON SEPT. 23, LEWIS AND CLARK GET BACK TO ST. LOUIS. LEWIS GOES ON TO WASHINGTON, D.C.

> WELCOME BACK, MERIWETHER! PEOPLE THOUGHT YOU WERE DEAD —YOU WERE GONE SO LONG!

> PRESIDENT JEFFERSON, WE TRAVELED 8,000 MILES. WE DISCOVERED 178 NEW PLANTS AND MET MANY INDIANS.

LEWIS ALSO DISCOVERED HOW TO TRAVEL WITHOUT SITTING ON HIS BEHIND!

END

CHAPTER 2

THE NATIONAL ROAD

Men who fought in the **American Revolution** were promised land west of the **Appalachian Mountains** in the **Ohio territory**. But how would they get there -- and to the new Louisiana Territory explored by **Lewis and Clark**? There was no easy way west in 1806. The paths were still narrow, winding Indian trails through the woods. **President Thomas Jefferson** had big dreams for the big lands over the mountains, but people needed a way to get there. . .

WAS A NATIONAL ROAD CONSTITUTIONAL?

IN THE OFFICE OF **PRESIDENT THOMAS JEFFERSON** IN 1806...

TERRIBLE ADVICE, TOM! TERRIBLE!! OUR CARRIAGE WHEELS BROKE TWICE ON OUR WAY TO SEE "NATURAL BRIDGE!" WE HAD TO CUT TREES TO MAKE A SLED TO CARRY THE CARRIAGE DOWN THE MOUNTAIN!!

WE BOUNCED OVER ROADS THAT WERE DREADFUL INDEED!

I APOLOGIZE, MADAME. TO SEE THE ROMANTIC INTERIOR OF OUR NEW UNITED STATES TAKES SOME... PATIENCE.

ISN'T "BRADDOCK'S ROAD" ONE OF YOUR BEST!?

YES, BUT IT IS STILL JUST A WIDENED INDIAN TRAIL. THE DELAWARE INDIAN **NEMACOLIN** BLAZED IT FOR THE OHIO COMPANY IN **1751**. THEN BRITISH GENERAL EDWARD BRADDOCK'S MEN USED IT IN THE FRENCH AND INDIAN WAR.

WELL, **FIX IT** OR AMERICA WILL **NEVER** BE A GREAT NATION!!

THEY'RE RIGHT, BUT I DON'T THINK THE FEDERAL GOVERNMENT HAS POWER TO DO THAT.

CONGRESS HAS PAID FOR LIGHTHOUSES AND BEACONS ON THE COAST TO BOOST TRADE WITH OTHER NATIONS! HOW IS BUILDING A ROAD ANY DIFFERENT?

CAPE HENRY LIGHTHOUSE VIRGINIA 1792

A LIGHTHOUSE SITS IN ONE STATE. A NATIONAL ROAD CROSSES STATE LINES. WE NEED AN AMENDMENT TO THE UNITED STATES CONSTITUTION TO BE ABLE TO DO THAT!

Constitution Roadmap for a New Government

CONGRESS JUST APPROVED THE CUMBERLAND ROAD ACT!

THAT'S RIGHT! THE PLAN TO BUILD A ROAD FROM **CUMBERLAND, MARYLAND**, TO THE WEST WAS MADE A FEW YEARS AGO WHEN OHIO WAS STILL A TERRITORY! THE FEDERAL GOVERNMENT CAN DO WHAT IT WANTS WITH **TERRITORIES!**

CHESTER, YOU'RE BRILLIANT!

JUST A CRAB DOING MY JOB, T.J.

next: ZANE

8

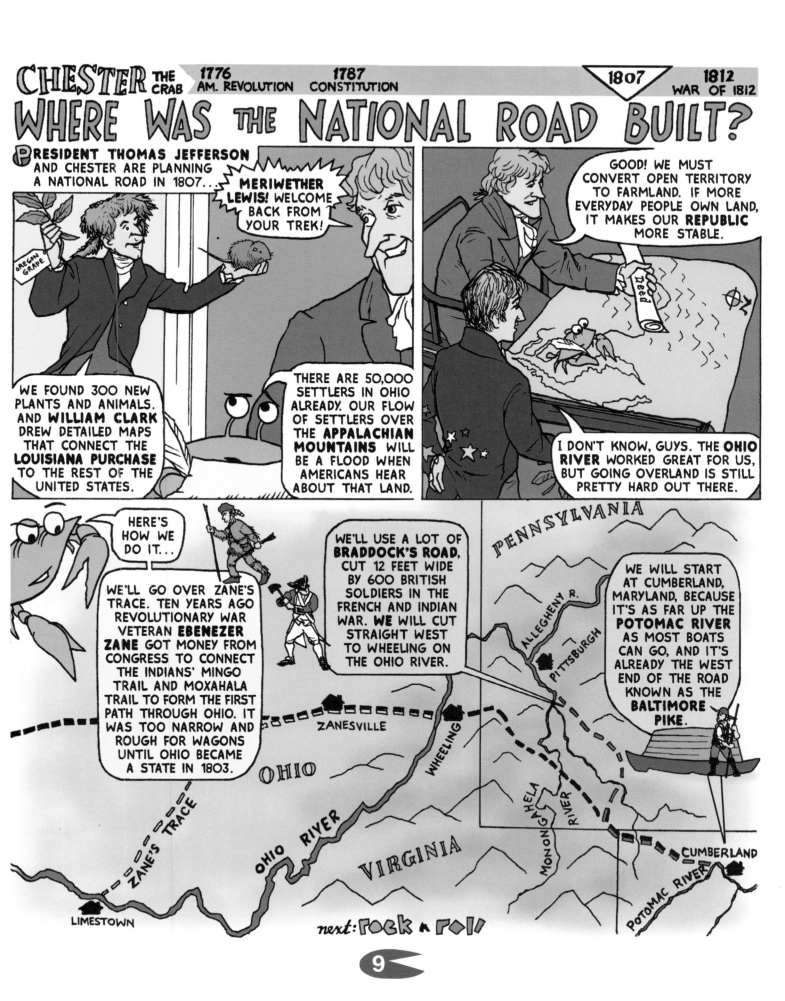

HOW WAS THE NATIONAL ROAD BUILT?

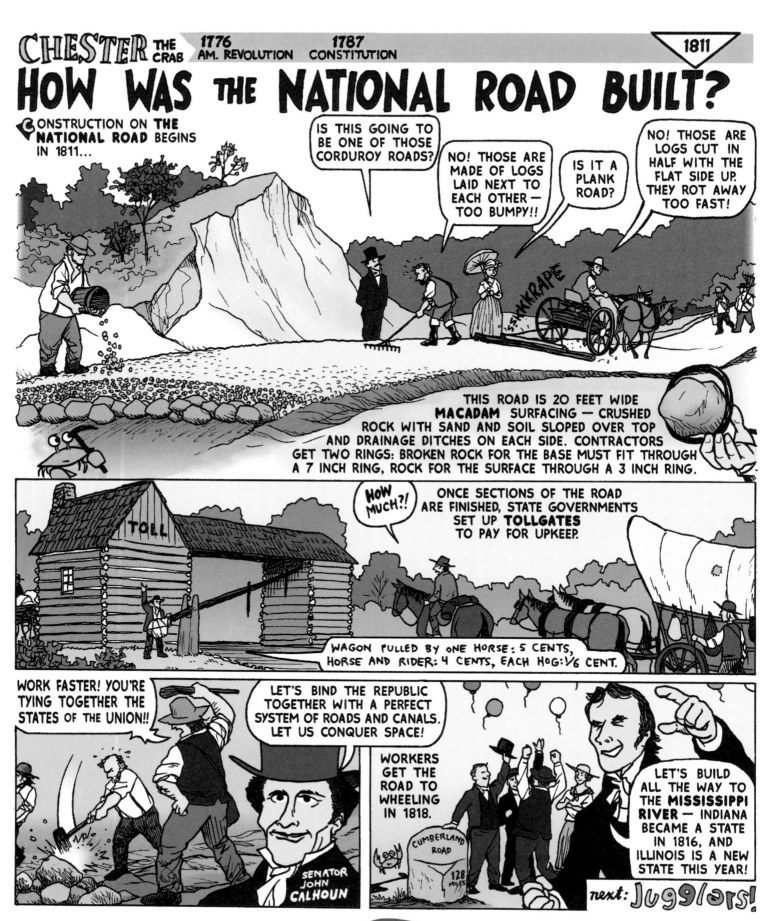

HOW WAS LIFE ALONG THE NATL. ROAD?

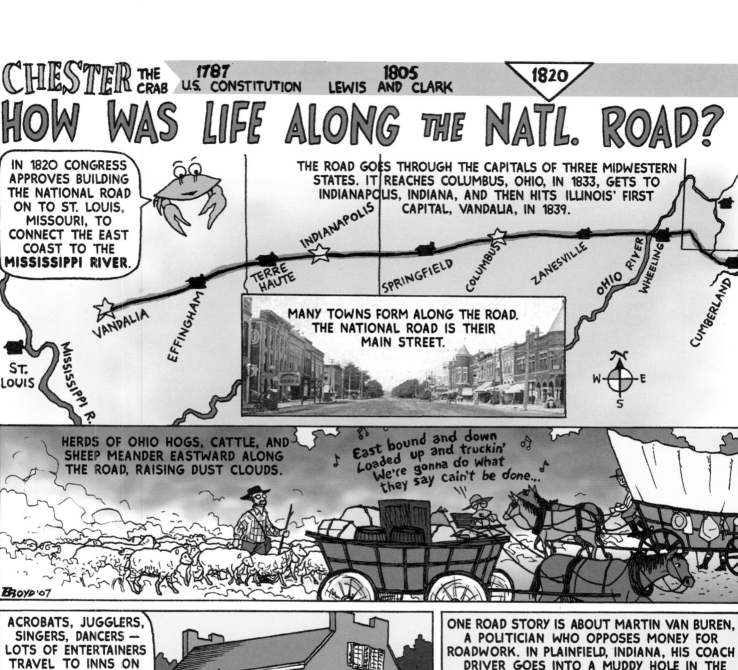

IN 1820 CONGRESS APPROVES BUILDING THE NATIONAL ROAD ON TO ST. LOUIS, MISSOURI, TO CONNECT THE EAST COAST TO THE **MISSISSIPPI RIVER.**

THE ROAD GOES THROUGH THE CAPITALS OF THREE MIDWESTERN STATES. IT REACHES COLUMBUS, OHIO, IN 1833, GETS TO INDIANAPOLIS, INDIANA, AND THEN HITS ILLINOIS' FIRST CAPITAL, VANDALIA, IN 1839.

MANY TOWNS FORM ALONG THE ROAD. THE NATIONAL ROAD IS THEIR MAIN STREET.

ST. LOUIS — MISSISSIPPI R. — VANDALIA — EFFINGHAM — TERRE HAUTE — INDIANAPOLIS — SPRINGFIELD — COLUMBUS — ZANESVILLE — OHIO RIVER — WHEELING — CUMBERLAND

W N E S

HERDS OF OHIO HOGS, CATTLE, AND SHEEP MEANDER EASTWARD ALONG THE ROAD, RAISING DUST CLOUDS.

♪ East bound and down
Loaded up and truckin'
We're gonna do what
they say cain't be done... ♪

BBOYD '07

ACROBATS, JUGGLERS, SINGERS, DANCERS — LOTS OF ENTERTAINERS TRAVEL TO INNS ON THE ROAD. THE ROAD CONNECTS SETTLERS WITH NEWS AND FUN FROM THE EAST COAST, FORMING AN AMERICAN POPULAR CULTURE.

AT THE RED BRICK TAVERN
Gen'l TOM THUMB
POSITIVELY FOR A SHORT TIME ONLY

ONE ROAD STORY IS ABOUT MARTIN VAN BUREN, A POLITICIAN WHO OPPOSES MONEY FOR ROADWORK. IN PLAINFIELD, INDIANA, HIS COACH DRIVER GOES INTO A MUDDY HOLE IN THE ROAD TO SHOW HIM THE NEED!

next:
RXR

WHY DID THE ROAD's POPULARITY FADE?

ARGUMENTS ABOUT THE CONSTITUTION DRAG NATIONAL ROADWORK DOWN. IN 1830 CONGRESS DEBATES BUILDING ANOTHER HIGHWAY FROM BUFFALO, NEW YORK, TO NEW ORLEANS. **PRESIDENT ANDREW JACKSON** VETOES THE PLAN AS PART OF A BROAD ROLLBACK OF **FEDERAL** POWERS.

CONSTRUCTION OF THE FIRST NATIONAL ROAD STOPS AT VANDALIA, ILLINOIS, IN 1839.

WELL, WE MADE IT 620 MILES...

IN 1840 CONGRESS VOTES AGAINST COMPLETING THE ROAD. BIG MONEY GOES TO **RAIL**ROAD CONSTRUCTION. (THE BALTIMORE AND OHIO RR GETS TO CUMBERLAND IN 1842 AND WHEELING IN 1853.)

AFTER THE CIVIL WAR THE NATIONAL ROAD FALLS INTO LOCAL PIECES — A DIRT RUT ACROSS THE MOUNTAINS, A QUIET LANE PAST OHIO FARMS.

CARS BRING BACK INTEREST IN THE ROAD. IN 1902 2,500 OLDSMOBILE CARS ARE SOLD AND THE NATIONAL ROAD FROM CUMBERLAND TO FROSTBURG, MARYLAND, IS RESURFACED. BY 1923 IT'S PAVED ALL THE WAY TO INDIANAPOLIS!

END

CHAPTER 3

FULTON'S STEAMBOAT

As some builders of the new nation worried about roads, others worried about water. For thousands of years, moving on rivers and oceans was the fastest way to get people and products from place to place. But there was one problem: moving **against** the flow of the water was hard. If only there was a machine that could push a boat against the current, the new United States could move a lot of people and products on its many rivers . . .

WHAT POWER CAME BEFORE STEAM POWER?

MANY YEARS AGO THERE WERE NO GASOLINE-POWERED TRUCKS, NO JET-ENGINE AIRPLANES, NO NUCLEAR POWER PLANTS MAKING ELECTRICITY. IF PEOPLE WANTED HEAVY WORK DONE, THEY HAD FEW CHOICES.

MUSCLE POWER

FROM HUMANS OR ANIMALS IS, FOR THOUSANDS OF YEARS, THE ONLY WAY TO BUILD THINGS. FOR EXAMPLE, IT TAKES ABOUT 100,000 PEOPLE 20 YEARS TO BUILD THE ANCIENT EGYPTIAN PYRAMIND CHEOPS FROM ABOUT SIX MILLION TONS OF STONE!

THE PROBLEM IS THAT MUSCLES CANNOT DO THE REALLY BIG STUFF FAST. AND MUSCLES GET TIRED AND NEED TO REST!

WIND POWER

BECOMES A USEFUL SOURCE OF ENERGY IN THE 600s IN ASIA. THE FIRST WINDMILL IN NORTH AMERICA IS BUILT IN 1621 AT FLOWERDEW HUNDRED IN VIRGINIA. THE TURNING SAILS MOVE GEARS TO CRUSH GRAIN FOR EASIER COOKING.

BROYD '03

THE PROBLEM IS NO WORK GETS DONE IF THE WIND STOPS!

HOW ABOUT FAIRY GODPOWER?

I'LL GET THE MONKEY!

WATER POWER

PUSHES THE GEARS OF MANY OTHER MILLS. THIS IS A POPULAR ENERGY SOURCE ON NORTH AMERICA'S EAST COAST BECAUSE THERE ARE SO MANY RIVERS.

WAAAA!

THE PROBLEM IS THAT THESE MILLS CAN ONLY SIT WHERE THERE IS FLOWING WATER.

WE NEED BIG POWER AT ANY TIME IN ANY PLACE...

NEXT: STEAMED CRAB

WHAT STEAMED JAMES WATT?

THE MODERN MACHINE AGE IS BASED IN PART ON IDEAS THAT FRENCH INVENTOR DENYS PAPIN FORMS IN THE LATE **1600**s

EARTH'S AIR HAS MATTER IN IT — TINY BITS OF THINGS WE CANNOT SEE.

THE MATTER IN AIR CAN PUT **PRESSURE** ON SOMETHING — SUCH AS ON A **VACUUM** (A SPACE COMPLETELY WITHOUT AIR OR MATTER).

Air

Vacuum

AIR PRESSURE PUSHES PISTON DOWN

STEAM IN CYLINDER PUSHES PISTON BACK UP

WATER HEATED IN BOILER

IN **1712** ENGLISHMAN THOMAS NEWCOMEN PUTS THESE IDEAS TO WORK. HE BUILDS AN ENGINE WITH PARTS MOVED BY AIR THAT HAS TINY, EXPANDING WATER DROPS IN IT — **STEAM!** NEWCOMEN'S MACHINE PUMPS WATER OUT OF DEEP MINES.

BOYD '03

NEWCOMEN'S MACHINE HAS MANY PARTS THAT OFTEN BREAK!

JAMES WATT! CAN YOU FIX THIS NEWCOMEN THINGY?

MAYTAG

WATT MAKES A BETTER STEAM ENGINE IN **1765** BY ADDING A SECOND CYLINDER. WATT'S ENGINE PRODUCES FOUR TIMES AS MUCH POWER AS THE NEWCOMEN ENGINE!

WHEN THIS PISTON RISES IT MAKES A VACUUM IN MAIN CYLINDER

CYLINDER

STEAM CASE

:GULP: BOILING WATER MAKES ME NERVOUS!

next: steam on the water...

WHO PUT STEAM POWER ONTO WATER?

PEOPLE GET EXCITED ABOUT WHAT **JAMES WATT'S** STEAM ENGINE CAN DO IN THE LATE **1700**s. CLOCKMAKER **JOHN FITCH** GETS A STEAM ENGINE TO MOVE 12 PADDLES ON THE DELAWARE RIVER DURING THE CONSTITUTIONAL CONVENTION IN 1787.

NOW BOATS DON'T HAVE TO WAIT FOR THE RIGHT WIND!

BUT WE'RE STILL WAITING TO GET ACROSS. YOUR BOAT IS SLOW!

FITCH'S BOAT ISN'T REVOLUTIONARY, BUT IT DOES TRAVEL 6,000 MILES UP AND DOWN THE DELAWARE BY 1790.

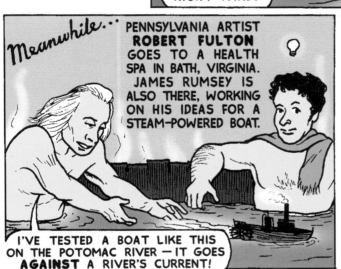

Meanwhile... PENNSYLVANIA ARTIST **ROBERT FULTON** GOES TO A HEALTH SPA IN BATH, VIRGINIA. JAMES RUMSEY IS ALSO THERE, WORKING ON HIS IDEAS FOR A STEAM-POWERED BOAT.

I'VE TESTED A BOAT LIKE THIS ON THE POTOMAC RIVER — IT GOES **AGAINST** A RIVER'S CURRENT!

FULTON GOES TO EUROPE TO STUDY ART BUT KEEPS DREAMING OF MACHINES. HE TRIES TO SELL FRANCE A SUBMARINE POWERED BY HAND CRANKS.

FULTON MEETS AMERICAN ROBERT LIVINGSTON.

I'LL MAKE A BOATLOAD OF MONEY IF I GET A 20-TON STEAMSHIP TO GO FOUR MILES AN HOUR!

FULTON BUILDS A STEAMBOAT FOR LIVINGSTON AND TESTS IT ON THE RIVER SEINE IN PARIS, FRANCE, IN 1803.

Oh NO!! THE FRENCH ENGINE IS TOO HEAVY!!

WHAT YOU NEED IS A **WATT!**

WATT STEAM ENGINES FROM ENGLAND ARE MUCH LIGHTER.

next: Steam Scene

HOW FAR DID STEAMBOATS GO?

ROBERT FULTON BUILDS 21 STEAMSHIPS DURING HIS LIFE. IN **1811** HIS "NEW ORLEANS" IS THE FIRST STEAMBOAT ON THE **MISSISSIPPI RIVER**.

DURING THE WAR OF 1812, FULTON BUILDS THE FIRST MODERN WARSHIP POWERED BY STEAM. IT IS NOT FINISHED IN TIME TO FIGHT THE WAR.

FULTON DIES IN 1815. THIS IS HIS LEGACY: HE DIDN'T MAKE THE FIRST STEAMSHIP, BUT HE MADE THEM EASY TO USE.

STEAMBOATS BECOME AN IMPORTANT PART OF AMERICAN BUSINESS.

THEY TAKE CROPS (TOBACCO, COTTON) FROM SOUTHERN STATES TO NORTHERN CITIES AND TAKE GOODS (FURNITURE, CLOTHES) FROM NORTHERN FACTORIES TO SOUTHERN FARMS.

STEAM HELPS MOVE AMERICA FASTER ON LAND, TOO.

STEAM TRAINS BEGIN CROSSING AMERICA IN THE 1830s. BY 1860 THERE ARE 30,000 MILES OF TRACK.

STEAM POWER CAN EVEN MOVE CARS! IN THE EARLY 1900s, "STANLEY STEAMERS" CHUG ALONG AMERICA'S ROADS.

END

THE ERIE CANAL

The National Road connecting the Ohio Valley to the Potomac River brought more wealth to the port city of **Baltimore**, Maryland. It didn't do much for the port of **New York City** or the rest of New York state to the north. Leaders there decided they must have their own gateway to the West, and they decided their gateway would be over water, not crushed rock . . .

WHERE WAS THE ERIE CANAL BUILT?

next: **ENGINEER SCHOOL**

HOW DID THEY CLEAR TREES FOR A CANAL?

CHESTER AND FIFTH-GRADER SAMUEL HAVE MET NEW YORK GOVERNOR DEWITT CLINTON IN **1820**...

WHY DO YOU WANT TO PUT A CANAL IN THE **WOODS**??

THIS WILL SPEED UP TRAVEL BETWEEN THE WESTERN FRONTIER AND THE EAST COAST. THERE ARE A LOT OF TREES BETWEEN THOSE TWO!

CUTTING THESE HUGE TREES BY HAND WOULD TAKE DECADES. BUT MY ENGINEERS BUILT A MACHINE THAT RIPS OUT 40 TREES A DAY!

RRRIP

"ENGINEERS?" THERE IS NO TRAIN HERE.

PEOPLE WHO DESIGN AND BUILD THINGS ARE ALSO CALLED ENGINEERS. AMERICA HAD NO ENGINEERS WHEN THIS CANAL BEGAN IN **1817**. THESE MEN ARE LEARNING ON THE JOB.

THE ENGINEERS MUST GET THROUGH SWAMPS...   CANYONS AND CLIFFS...   ...AND OVER RIVERS.

Whoops!

HOW WILL WE BUILD A WATER HIGHWAY **OVER** A RIVER??

IF YOU CAN SOLVE THAT, YOU WILL MAKE THIS CANAL "AMERICA'S FIRST SCHOOL OF ENGINEERING."

next: AQUA DUCKS

WHAT DOES AN AQUEDUCT CARRY?

CHESTER AND FIFTH-GRADER SAMUEL ARE WATCHING THE CONSTRUCTION OF THE **ERIE CANAL**.

BRITISH-CONTROLLED **LAKE ONTARIO**

OK, GOVERNOR CLINTON, WHAT **NOW**? YOUR CANAL GOING EAST AND WEST HAS HIT THE GENESEE RIVER GOING NORTH AND SOUTH.

ROCHESTER

I'D RATHER BE "RAW CHESTER" THAN STEAMED CHESTER!

GENESEE RIVER

NEW YORK

CANANDAIGUA

CANVASS WHITE, YOU ARE MY ENGINEER. WHAT DO WE DO?

BORROW A PAGE FROM ANCIENT ROME! WE BUILD AQUEDUCTS (BRIDGES CARRYING WATER) OVER THE RIVERS AND VALLEYS ALONG THE CANAL PATH.

WORK BEGINS ON AN AQUEDUCT THROUGH DOWNTOWN ROCHESTER, NEW YORK.

DID YOU KNOW "AQUA" IS LATIN FOR WATER, AND "DUCTUS" MEANS LEADING?

I KNOW THIS IS COSTING **MILLIONS** OF DOLLARS!!

WHEN IT IS FINISHED, THE AQUEDUCT OVER THE GENESEE RIVER IS 802 FEET LONG. IT IS THE LONGEST STONE BRIDGE IN AMERICA AT THE TIME.

NEXT: WATERFALLS

HOW DO YOU LOWER A CANAL BOAT?

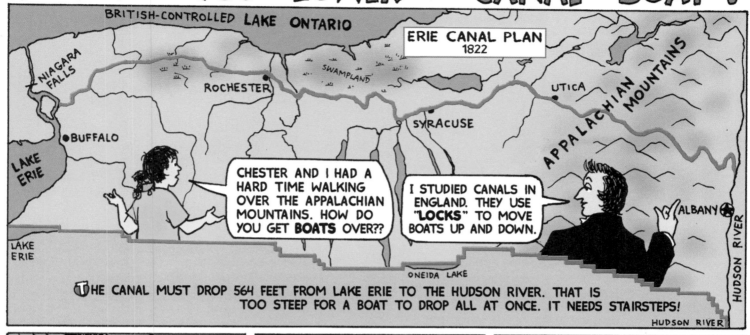

BRITISH-CONTROLLED LAKE ONTARIO

ERIE CANAL PLAN 1822

NIAGARA FALLS • ROCHESTER • SWAMPLAND • UTICA • SYRACUSE • BUFFALO • LAKE ERIE • ONEIDA LAKE • ALBANY • HUDSON RIVER • APPALACHIAN MOUNTAINS • LAKE ERIE

CHESTER AND I HAD A HARD TIME WALKING OVER THE APPALACHIAN MOUNTAINS. HOW DO YOU GET **BOATS** OVER??

I STUDIED CANALS IN ENGLAND. THEY USE **"LOCKS"** TO MOVE BOATS UP AND DOWN.

THE CANAL MUST DROP 564 FEET FROM LAKE ERIE TO THE HUDSON RIVER. THAT IS TOO STEEP FOR A BOAT TO DROP ALL AT ONCE. IT NEEDS STAIRSTEPS!

HUDSON RIVER

BBOYD '01

A LOCK IS A BOX WITH DOORS ON EACH END. THE DOOR AGAINST THE HIGHER WATER OPENS TO LET A BOAT AND WATER IN.

THE UPPER DOOR CLOSES. WATER IN THE LOCK SLOWLY DRAINS OUT HOLES SO THE BOAT CAN GO DOWN AS THE WATER GOES DOWN.

THEN THE DOOR AGAINST THE LOWER WATER IS OPENED, AND THE BOAT CONTINUES ON THE CANAL.

WHAT WILL WE BUILD **83** LOCKS OUT OF?! WOOD ROTS. CEMENT THAT HARDENS UNDERWATER CAN ONLY BE BOUGHT IN EUROPE. IT'S TOO EXPENSIVE!

THAT EUROPEAN CEMENT HAS PUMICE IN IT. WHERE CAN WE FIND PUMICE IN AMERICA??

I THINK I STUMBLED INTO SOME OVER YONDER.

THE NEXT DAY. . .

LOOK! THE STUFF CHESTER FOUND HARDENED IN WATER OVERNIGHT! WE CAN MAKE CEMENT HERE!!

ROCK CRABSTER !!

next: *Wedding the Waters*